IAMHERE

TALIN ESH

B"H

I
Am
Here

Talin Esh

B"H

I AM HERE

Copyright ©2024 by Talin Esh

All rights reserved.

No part of this book may be reproduced or transmitted in any form or by any means without written permission of the author. In the case of brief quotations embodied in critical articles and reviews, reproduction is permissible with proper citation and notification.

To contact Talin Esh for speaking arrangements, please email lifecanbetalin@gmail.com

ISBN 978-0-9916196-2-7

Library of Congress Control

Printed in the United States of America

Lifecanbe Press
Cover Original Work by Rudolph Leder – RMRVI

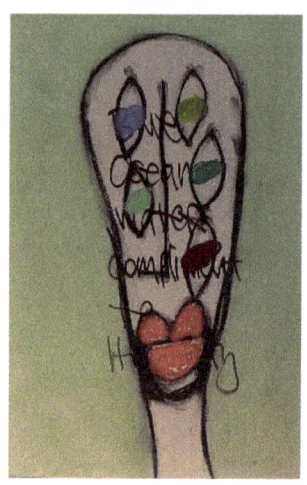

A message from the Artist…

I call these works "Reflections." Each piece offers a glimpse into the present moment, capturing feelings, colors, and emotions as they unfold.

"Echoes of Humanity" refers to the resonant and enduring aspects of what it means to be human.

Feelings: Blue, Ocean, Water, Compliment to Humanity, Green, Duality.

"Rudolph Leder – RMRVI"

B"H

Dedication

For my children. Thank you for teaching me what it means to love. I give you all I am.

What is poetry…

Poetry is the art of living in words and finding its way through the unknown. An unseen image revealed in a way mysterious yet plain, only you can see the meaning that is meant for you. In the words of Bob Dylan, "I don't know how I got to write those songs, they were almost magically written." "I did it at one time." "You can't do something forever, I got to do it, once. I can do other things now… I can't do that." He ended, on an interview with Ed Bradley on 60 minutes.

Bob Dylan, an inspiration, describes what most poets do, and who they are at their core, the essence of their craft. There is a magic to writing poetry. It comes through us, not from us. That is because it is not about us, but we are simply put- the mediums, the distributors, the channel. We use all we know to deliver the message. It's humbling and relieving at the same time. To be an artist is to know the creator intimately. To be certain and in awe & disbelief all at the same moment in time. It is to surrender to the creator in its creation within ourselves, to be grounded in truth of the universe.

"What would life be worth living for, if not the beauty we find in it that which brings a flutter to the heart and warmth to our soul." I bring you these simple words of a humble poet, your guide into the beauty you seek.

B"H

CONTENTS

TITLE PAGE ………………………………..3

A MESSAGE FROM THE ARTIST ………..4

DEDICATION …………….……………….5

CONTENTS ……………………………..6-8

POET'S CORNER ……………….……..9-10

POETRY

A MOTHER'S TOUCH

    I.   #BLESSED ………………………… 14
    II.   #ONCEUPONATIME ……………… 15
    III.   #BRANDNEWDAY ………………… 16
    IV.   #AMOTHERSPRAYER ……….…... 17-18
    V.   #IAMYOURMOTHER ……….…… 19
    VI.   #MAMA ……………………………. 20
    VII.   #MORETIME ………………..…….. 21
    VIII.   #SHOULDHAVEKNOWN …………. 22
    IX.   #ALWAYSWITHYOU……….…...…. 23
    X.   #MILLENNIALS ……...…..……….. 24-25
    XI.   #ABETTERTOMORROW …………. 26

A NATION'S LOVE

    XII.   #FREEIRAN …………………….…. 30
    XIII.   #IAMANAMERICAN ………………. 31
    XIV.   #MYFLAG …………………………. 32
    XV.   #MIGHTY …………………………..33
    XVI.   #IAMMAHSA… ……………………. 34

B"H

    XVII.   #BORROWEDTIME ....…........ 35
    XVIII. #FLAWED ………..…................ 36

A FRIEND'S HOLD

    XIX.   #FREEDOMME ....…........... 40
    XX.   #HELLO ……...................…..….. 41
    XXI.   #HAPPYBIRTHDAY...................... 42
    XXII.   #LEAVEONLYFOOTPRINTSBEHIND.... 43
    XXIII. #LIBERATION ....…....…..... 44
    XXIV. #TRANSPARENCY….................... 45

AN ENEMY'S RELEASE

    XXV.   #CLEAR ………...................... 48
    XXVI.   #CHAINEDTOSLAVERY 49
    XXVII. #COLLECTINGSTONES 50
    XXVIII. #ESCORTTOTHETOP ….............. 51
    XXIX.   #THEDECREE ....…... 52
    XXX.   #THEFINALFALL ….................... 53
    XXXI.   #GLASSCEILINGS ….................... 54

A HOME'S PAIN

    XXXII.   #DYSFUNCTIONAL .....….......... 58
    XXXIII. #WORDSMATTER ……............... 59
    XXXIV. #BECAUSEICOULDNOTLOVE…... 60
    XXXV.   #FEAR ………....................…..... 61

A JOURNEY'S END

    XXXVI.   #FEARNOTI…..................…..... 64
    XXXVII. #YOURLIFETOO ....…....….. 65
    XXXVIII. #UNIVERSE ....…............ 66
    XXXIX.   #SEE ....….. 67
    XL.   #SPEAKUP…...............…........ 68
    XLI.   #CHALLENGEACCEPTED 69

B"H

XLII.	#SAVETHEDAY	70
XLIII.	#MYHERO	71
XLIV.	#LIFEISFORTHELIVING	72
XLV.	#TIME	73
XLVI.	#CREATION	74
XLVII.	#THEHOUROFDEATH	75

A SOUL'S TRUTH

XLVIII.	#MEMORIES	78
XLIX.	#SURVIVOR	79
L.	#FREEDOM	80
LI.	#TOBUILDORBRAKE	81
LII.	#CHALLENGEMENOT	82
LIII.	#BROKENTOGETHER	83
LIV.	#LESSONLEARNED	84
LV.	#RICHES	85
LVI.	#IAMHERE	86

ABOUT THE POET 88-89
FINAL WORDS 90
ACKNOWLEDGEMENTS 92

Poet's Corner

The opportunity to say thank you is like a royal coronation. The ability to stand proud and share of gratitude because my cup overflow'th. There were many people who supported me to bring this collection alive. In the words of Snopp Dogg, "first and foremost, I must thank myself. I want to thank me for believing in me, I want to thank me for doing all this hard work, … I want to thank me for never quitting, …." I say it in jest but also with love. It has been a journey to learn to appreciate myself. A never-ending voyage to dive into the depths of my mind and to work on myself, bringing out raw emotion, unfiltered and yet ready to share with the world. Despite all my fears of shame, fear of vulnerability, and fear of judgement; to find the courage to share it with the world is my hope to inspire all.

That courage did not come on it's own. It was the support and love of the people around me who believed in me when I didn't believe in myself; the people who loved me when I didn't have the energy to love myself and most especially people who trusted me when I was flying high in doubt. I cannot forget the people who put me down so hard so that only I could pick myself back up. So I thank *you* too. Learning the necessary lesson of life that no one is coming to save and you must stand for yourself is the springboard into living a fulfilled life.

It is uncommon in our world, but with openness and connection and a willingness to be real it is possible for everyone. We are all made up of our ancestors' universe combined with our own interpretations of the images we process in this physical world. When we realize that and begin to unattach from what is false in our head, only then can we connect to each other and generate love in it's truest form.

My teammate, Michael Hussain carries the very essence of that. A powerful, generator of love. I would have not shared my poetry if it wasn't for his encouragement. So I thank him sincerely. In

B"H

another world we were destined to be enemies, raised to hate and to fear one another. But in this world we connect, embrace and support. We carry one another forward and upward. How lucky am I to have you walk in through my life.

How to say thank you to my husband who stands by my everyday's? The happy, the ugly, the sad, the dull and plain days... My love, my partner, the one who choose me above all others to create a family with and the one who I choose everyday since to create a life. My dear husband PJ. I am all I am because of the love, support and space you give me, to be who I want to be. There are challenges in married life, in traditional societies and many fear driven limitations that inhibit the growth of oneself and one another. We confront those obstacles and while at time we may submit, in more times we work through the challenges and come out enlightened on the other side.

This book could not exist if I was not given the space to discover within myself and given the liberty to share it with the world. My love leaves the door open for me to explore and express on my own without judgement nor limitations. In another lifetime, there would have been too much fear restraining such self-expression but I'm blessed to be in this lifetime with you. Thank you. Ebbyjoon, you are confident, loving and supporting – this book is as much your accomplishment as it is my words. You have given me a lifetime of possibilities. iluvu.

B"H

B"H

'birth'

A MOTHER'S TOUCH

#blessed

I sit with you upon my chest
Minutes pass to hours in a blink of an eye
No where else do I wish to rest
Knowing now Precious is this time

Perfection is your little nose
And lips to die for
Your eyes gateway to the heavens
And hands I already adore

Are you any different
Or am I
As I enjoy every minute of you
I learn the latter

I inhale your beauty
Exhale your being
Embrace your touch
Admire your perfect creation

No question
You are a gift from above
Everyday a miracle
In every way an act of Gd.

#onceuponatime

Once upon a time
I used to recite your favorite rhymes
Your hand in mine I did adore
Hours passed before I know

Once upon a time
Your head upon my chest
Never giving a moment's rest
In a whisper I would dine
Once upon a time

Once upon a time
I knew so clear how much I loved you
To the moon and back we read together
Little did i know it would not last forever

Once upon a time
They said enjoy this time for it will end
Secretly I thought but when
Did they not know how tired I was then

Once upon a time
It was true
the door closed and out came the words I hate you
Shattered I fell to my knees every time
But love, love will you please be kind

Once upon a time
I recalled the days that were mine
I gave them space to feel it out
And wouldn't you know they came back

Once upon a time
Each moment is divine
Pain and glory alike
Love like this... you can not find.

#brandnewday

it is a glorious new day
every time you awake
midnight hours our own
no others to take

I cherish these moments for they last too few
the winds blow hard outside us
but you are safe inside my embrace
no others to take

amazement has not even a chance
at this great miracle at hand
believers i seek not fate
no others to take

alone you and I
utopia in my eye
midnight hours our own
no others to take

#amother'sprayer

I pray you know your worth despite when I say no
I pray you know you are loved despite when I don't say so
I pray you know you are always welcome despite when you close the door
I pray you know laughter from your soul but know tears also have a purpose for.

May you have good people around you,
even when I don't agree
May you choose better in times of strife,
when life brings you to your knees
May you find your passion and your purpose
in everything you do
May you leave the world a better place
just by being who is you.

Life is passing Nothing stays the same
What is here today might remain
tomorrow it will eventually find its way
Temporary moments don't make for final decisions
Always have an exit but don't always score it
Trust in people and be present to their actions
Never fear to walk away but more importantly
never fear to stay.

Life is hard but it is also beautiful
People will hurt you and they will love you
Nobody is perfect, don't expect it from others
Expectations only end in your disappointment,

B"H

Nobody is perfect, don't expect it from yourself
Do your best and that will always be enough
Forgive your mistakes, learning from them is what's tough
Be open to thinking differently
and please always speak your truth
Speak to G-d often and let faith guide you through.

Challenges, troubles, smiles and grief
It's what makes a life complete
There is no way around it
The choice is up to you
to smile and still say please.

Forgive me for my mistakes
I too am not perfect
Still learning healing & growing
from my own story's circuits
One thing is true from the minute you were conceived
I love you,
more than even I can believe.

B"H

#iamyourmother

I AM YOUR MOTHER HEAR ME ROAR
I WILL BEG BORROW AND STEAL
TO SEE YOU SOAR

I AM YOUR MOTHER HEAR ME ROAR
DON'T LET THE TEARS FOOL YOU
I WILL PUSH YOU MORE

I AM YOUR MOTHER HEAR ME ROAR
TO SEE YOU EXCEL
IS MY ULTIMATE GOAL

I AM YOUR MOTHER HEAR ME ROAR
IT MAY HURT NOW
BUT TOMORROW I'LL BE GONE

I AM YOUR MOTHER HEAR ME ROAR
I PREPARE YOU AS BEST I CAN
EVEN IF YOU THINK I'M WRONG

I AM YOUR MOTHER HEAR ME ROAR
IF YOU MESS UP then FESS UP
I'LL LOVE YOU MORE

I AM YOUR MOTHER HEAR ME ROAR
LOVE ME OR NOT
I'LL LOVE YOU FOR
I AM YOUR MOTHER HEAR ME ROAR

#mama

I wake by a sound filled with fright
I creep quickly like a thief in the night
Joyfully I watch the precious souls asleep
Amazed I am here for them to keep

I check each one for breath and light
Lucky am I to have such a sight
Their little bodies resting peacefully
Grateful G-d gave you to me

Wonder us of what lies ahead
Your life so bright and full

I want to guide you
Letting go will be hard to do
But it is your path to pave
Worry I not, you will be brave

Happy mother's day indeed
But it is to you I say not you to me
Thank you for choosing me
This gift is all I need

#Moretime

My cup overflow'th
With glory and pain
But complain do not I dare

For worse I can't bare
Life so short but my day so long
Grin and bear it I try
My child with others time spent
What more can I rent

I watch the minute but the hours I did not see
I rush and consolidate but where's my efficiency
More time I need
More time I need

Try and perfect
Try and repeat
Where have I gone
Where have I been

Same journey same glory
Over and over and over again
Tell me when will this end
When will happy I see again.

#Shouldhaveknown…

A mother stands by
    watching her child
  wanting to do more than
help
  wanting to tie the lace without a knot
  wanting to ride the bike without a fall
But the child must be the one
    to go on.

It's hard for a mother
  to see the child suffer
And it's harder for the child
  to see the mother tougher
But both know what must happen.

And to let this happen

A mother must let go
    For with out that fall
The child won't grow.

The child being on it's own self now
  It's hard not to take the wrong path out
With this in mind
A mother should have known
  How could she have let
  her child go.

Mistakes are made by all
by mother and child both
It's part of our faults of being human
It's part of our burden to accept it.

#alwayswithyou

You are my children but not mine to keep
I have a job so honored you chose me
You are my blessings but not my retreat
I see you as you are and I see me

Like rocks washed ashore
We arrive together
Where you will go
That you will tether
How you will get there
I do not know
But right beside you
I will be

My love is boundless, unconditional
Challenges maybe not quite typical

Darkness has its ways in, you will find
Know your light inside, Infinite and divine
You are a part of what I did, that was right.

#millennials

i wonder the next generation
and how they can go so wrong
so i think back to how it all begun
it is not all their fault
we as parents did it to them
so some blame we must take
in mothering them

we got slapped around
so we swore we wouldn't hit
instead we gave meaningless trophies
even when they didn't win
don't cry my baby
you are the best
even when you don't take the test

we were controlled
always told what to do
so instead we gave up
all orders and nouns
now the hes and shes
only be found at the zoo

strangers around us
make us whole
while those close
have no love at all

greed and deception
tipping the scales
the source only a theory
never to be named
while those who believe
a minority holding the shame

we are just at the opposite end
of where we started
no real movement at all
progression i think not
just the other side of the same straw

we made it to the bottom
where all the grime lays
now it's in the hands
of these poor millennials
to make it rain.

#abettertomorrow

Lucky for some I am ignorant
Lucky for some I am not.
Lucky for some I am inexperienced
Lucky for some I am not.

My day's journey bring always a slice of hope
That one day man will be kind
Today is not that day
But the hope has not yet died.

The end is an undeniable fact for all.
But all too soon for the innocence
Or maybe we just don't know
Its God's way of calling his good children home.

The end I do not fear
But leaving my children behind
In this place where no one cares
Of what is good and what is right.

But I make my bed as the general said
And continue my day one task done
Only to see the tortures we bring
For in the end greed has won.

But there is still hope
For everyday I wake a new
If God believes we can be good
Then choices we make can be too.

B"H

'in between'

B"H

A NATION'S LOVE

#FREEIRAN

You shoot your guns with some blanks
And maybe bullets that hurt my hand
But every shot over my head
makes my voice louder heard

You are paid by my blood
Terror can only last a some
As time passes fear abides
And despite my fear hands arise

You are out numbered
your baton hurt no more
Children I dare not give you
until I settle the score

44 years you took my life
My country stands with my wife
No longer will I stand behind
While you feed my men with your lies.

#iamanamerican

what tears roll down your cheek my friend
is it for the lives you lost
is it for the stores burned down
is it for the childhood robbed of it's innocence

no you say
for the clouds to come
are much more grey
chaves, castro, khomeani, won

we are all in turn for the next
i cry for the battles held in text
the war of words that truth had none
no matter the mayor smiled and run

it was today at 10 years old,
tested i was to be told
american you are and now you hold
the greatest country unfold.

B"H

#myflag

For this flag
    I would stand proud
For this flag
    I would always defend it
For this flag
    is not perfect
For this flag
    has only one sound
For this flag
    I am grateful
For this flag
    took great pain
For this flag
    I will know not any other
For this flag
    willing to change
For this flag
    has many flaws
For this flag
    knows it well
For this flag
    to stand proud despite it
For this flag
    brings a unified strength

For this flag … can't do it alone
For this flag … vulnerable at its core
For this flag … needs goodness behind it
For this flag … otherwise will fall.

#mighty

Today i cry
When i was meant to laugh
I cry for my brother
The solider protecting my life
I cry for he cannot
He stands proud gun in hand
Facing death straight on
A simple star on his heart
Instead of tears
blood pours his brow
Instead of dancing
He is underground

Today it started
The war against us
They didn't know how mighty
We are in trust
He steps in towards the flame
While we run away
My brother i feel your boil shaking
I can't wish your aching fade away
take the reins
tell me where to go
under this blanket of security
you have gifted me
my vote,
Will that set you free?

#iammahsa

Mahsa joon
What have they done to you?
The country calls out your name
But not a single cry of shame

My heart is with you
As you soar to heaven
Too early you have left us
your score a perfect seven

At the hand of gashte ershad
They will try to cover
Create a story
Where they have done no wrong

You we see beyond the veil
Your name we call beyond the rein
I am Mahsa born and free.
I am Mahsa
Let me be.

#borrowedtime

This is for the children of today
We are sorry for how we behaved
We stopped speaking with God
Instead we worked with no love

Then the bills started to soar
Coming in from our days with more
Confused where it all went
We said last will be to pay our rent

We live on but borrowed time
And now we add a borrowed dime
We taught you freedom above all else
And to focus on thyself

And now we learned our parents were right
It was not for the party we had to fight
The red white and the blue
Are the colors of the truth

We will leave you soon
Passing the baton without a clue
On your own will you build a new
America is counting on you

#flawed

i wonder to myself
why there is so much hatred in the world
i remember it is because we are human
we are flawed
we must work, removing the hatred
it is hard
we are lazy
it is so much easier to hate
today we are reminded to be grateful
grateful for all our haves and not focus on our have nots
what's most important we have not
we have not peace in this world
our hatred is killing our brothers and sisters
it is no one's fault except for that merely
we are human
we must accept our flaws
accept ourselves
no one person is right, no one person is wrong
buddhist, christian, muslim, jewish... atheist
all just yearning to be loved
but no one willing to do the loving
wasting time on proving a point
of who is right and who is wrong
while my brother lays on the ground
bleeding back into the earth
all just to do it again

B"H

'healer'

B"H

A FRIEND'S HOLD

#Freedomme

FREEDOMME...
I won't let you down
I only ask for you support
in order to prevent my fall

If you see me trip
I only ask for your hand
to have a strong grip

I only ask that you advise,
not to tell me any lies

If you speak of truth
I only ask that you
see me through

I only ask for some space
so I can feel for another taste

If you can't see me be
I only ask of you that
you set me free!

#Hello...

Life passes some of us by
   only living, us to die.
But when there's the one who stands
   We wake from the clapping hands.

A wake up call for some.
For others one who is bothersome.
Without which one could easily go on.
Without which life is quite a lonely one.

Life passes some of us by
   Grateful of that when we are caught in a lie.
But for when the end comes near
   We wonder why for all those tears.

A wake up call, a bit late for some.
Now there's not much more to be won.
Without which the end would have been quite in vain.
Without which, ignorance would have spared some pain.

B"H

#happybirthday

A love story that started in seventh grade.
So many memories have been made.
Easy, dizzy, humming, Skids galore,
prank calls, phone books and so much more.

Sleepovers and 'sweet sixteens'
never can forget the moments in-between
other friends have come and gone forth
breaks we've taken, space for growth.

A love like ours, unbreakable
always holding a truth be told.
A listening ear, a shoulder to brace
whatever is coming across our face.

Our differences could not be further apart
but also what brings close in heart.

Mistakes we've made and forgiveness came
my gratitude for you forever ingrained.

Happy birthday my dear dear friend
I love you forever and then again.

B"H

#leaveonlyfootprintsbehind

To those who love me
Thank you, you fill my heart
To those who let me love them
Thank you, you make me whole

To those who care for me
Thank you, you give me hope
To those who I get to care for
Thank you, you give me reason to stay

To those who call my name
Thank you, You give me kinship
To those I call your name
Thank you, You give me friendship

To those who gaze upon my eyes
Thank you, You give my soul breath
To those who hurt me beyond lies
Thank you, You give my soul work

I come to this world with nothing in hand
I leave alone the same way
Only lessons learned and GODs plan
Gratitude for my stay.

#liberation

People often ask me
how I'm so free?
Being truthful and authentic,
is liberating.
No mask displayed
for you
means
no energy wasted
making a mask
for me.
No one can never
fault me
of not being honest,
not being me.
who am I?
still to find
the truth is
if you have to ask
I'm not your kind.

#Transparency

If only your boots could talk of your style
and that walk through those streets
that fatally burn
to the point of no return

One step over a jump
I guess you could call it just a hunch
Discovery of a lifetime
Without recognition of any vision

You choose your steps
carefully
but jumped where ever
you were free.
Without thought
they looked at you
without fault
you turned them blue.

Never could otherwise do
Not your turn
Not your reason to
Strap on those boots
Don't look back
One day others will follow your tracks

B"H

'surrender'

AN ENEMY'S RELEASE

#clear

This is the day
my vision is so clear. I see it.
I see it right away.

This is the time that I can't replace.
These are the days that I must live
For the hour,
For the second,
For the time,
For time is not here to stay.

Time is of the essence.
What essence that may be.
We all do not know.
For we are born without a sole.
A sole is what we reach at our death.
A soul is what goes on beyond our stay.

Who is to know
What we show is true
Who is to feel
that our heart's turned blue

Now is the time.
So that we see, our fellow rise.
And now is the time
that we see our fellow fall.
Do we lend out a hand, to reach those from the ground?
Do we raise our hand, to be picked off the floor?
Where is this floor?
We are not to know, born without a sole.
But for those above us, for sure they will show.

#chainedtoslavery

You alone know only what you think you know.

The truth can only be seen once you let go of all your current beliefs.

Let go of all the lies you were told and all the lies you told yourself.

Judgment is for fools and no one else.

War is for nonbelievers who falsely believe they control the world.

Truth is saved only for the enlightened of this universe.

Be careful when you walk down Park Avenue,

your mind has been altered by false narratives that leave you empty inside, void of anything of value.

Only the truth will set you free of the bondage and slavery you have chained yourself to.

B"H

#collectingstones

I've traveled far and wide
only to come back to where I started
Lessons learned but some forgotten
Destiny not one from which to hide

Our glory is not one of our own
But rather gifts from which we grow
Our pain is not of punishment you see
But of leaps of faith to show and be

Challenge was to get to this place
And now the ride is on to space
I have my faith in tact and calm
Where to my friend, no alarm.

You are stuck in your stones collected
Spending hours and dollars suspected
Counting sheep but no calm sleep
For tired you are of this keep

I pray for you
One day you find
This piece of mind
Peace in time.

#escorttothetop

A lesson learned is a scar that's healed
Tender to the touch and beautiful to reveal
A powerful embrace taught by life itself
Never wonder why but laugh in its place

Tears have grown forests while compliments raised none
Muscles torn and tattered broke them down just in the name of fun
Fires torched the remains of nothingness lands barren
But in the heat explodes a new life to come

Destruction with itself brings life
It's just to where you look, dark or light
Choice is yours for the chance to take
Let life in or perhaps take a break

There is no right. There is no wrong.
Happiness is just another moment to spare
Tell me what dear have you collected?
Is there anyone who will escort you there?

#thedecree

There are our hopes and dreams and then there is reality.
Often unaligned, usually a result of our own decree,
and always an act of G-d.
The question is not in why? but in how or what is left to be done -
or sometimes undone.
To answer one must first understand - knowledge -
the knowing of the unknown.
There lies the quintessential dilemma as
too few of us actually understand.
Taught from day one to do as we are told,
to follow the lead of those we are instructed to hold.
Apprehended if we strayed the trust, like sheep to a slaughter we prayed,
we followed a path directed to us.

Some, oblivious of the destination ahead enjoyed the journey along the way.
Others, too focused on the end - missed all
in between heaven sent.
And some, some very, very few, find a new route
all together to spend.
While they too will pass somewhere someday –
it will not be at the hands of their prey.

#thefinalfall

what to do when the words are not true
do you yell and scream or sit still and pray
secrets portrayed a different way
truth came out and it's all for you

vultures up top and scavengers below
sitting still no longer prey
trouble came when i went away
now they can feed with the crows

is it i who fell
alliances made and favors paid
no one else to stand in their way
only time will tell

one speaks up
only chatter surrounds
loyalty has no ground
one falls down

#glassceilings

Breaking glass ceilings all around.
Not just me but with you in hand
This journey we were meant to climb
The steepest mountain we could find

Each step carefully placed
Sometimes lost sometimes haste
But even through all those mistakes
A smile you bring upon my face

We are not but enemies swear
Characters we are to carry the dare
Frightened but never lonely
For each other we hold holy

Chances are you were to hurt
Not I to hold the blame
Forever not to carry
Forever not in pain.

B"H

'rumination'

B"H

A HOME'S PAIN

B"H

#Dysfunctional

The sirens go round and round,
The lights roar fiercely out loud.
There is a problem, my love,
One that I am sure of,
One that all don't understand

Not even the one who is always around.
The lights attract attention
The sirens call from every dimension
Problems unsure with no solution
Nor a cure, not even one to mention
Commotion so meaningless with time wasted.
There is so much tension, even I could taste it.

The siren I don't wait to see
The light I don't want to hear
But all are always around me
And much too much too near

I just want to go home, I hear them say
While there is where the problem started its way.

#wordsmatter

Words cannot hurt but they destroy
Words cannot do but they inspire to
Words are simple but they complicate
Words are true but too often misused

A life with many words is scattered
A life with few words is pure
A life of kind words is ordained
A life of harsh words is confused

Understanding is offered in words
Confusion is offered in words too
Pain is offered in words are offered in pain
Forgiveness is offered in vain

Life is not without hardship is not without life
Solutions are not without problems are not without solutions
Words are not without strife

Givers are not without takers are not without givers
Love is not without pain is not without love
Words are not without fervor is not without words

#BecauseIcouldnotLove....

Because I could not love I was alone
Because I could not love I had no home
Because I could not love I sat by the ledge
Because I could not love I had the edge

Because I could not love
  I didn't understand the power
Because I could not love
  I didn't just pass the hour
Because I could not love
  No one could love me
Because I could not love
  Know I not what to see.

#Fear

I fear to like you
Because you may go
I fear to like you because you may stay
I fear to like you because you may stray
I fear to like you because you may fade

I fear to like you because there are reasons
I fear to like you because there are none
I fear to like you because I may cry
I fear to like you because you make me smile
I fear to like you because they may talk
I fear to like you because you will then walk
I fear to like you because then I'll want
I fear to like you because forced I to hunt
I fear to like you for the pleasures you bring
I fear to like you will cause me to sin
I fear to like you because the day you will not call
I fear to like you because I will fall
I fear to like you for the day you make me wait
I fear to like you for I may care so much to hate
I fear to like you for you may be so real
I fear to like you for this ease so surreal

I fear to like you because you may stay
I fear to like you
because you may go away.

B"H

'broken heart builds wings'

B"H

A JOURNEY'S END

#fearnoti

I do not fear death
I fear that I have not lived

Not wonder I, where lies go
wonder what Truth reveals standing still

It is short this life of ours
99 years to span the earth

I have seen but smiles and sours
Pictures taken, dead at birth

Journey ended, that is all
Grave dug, buried a covered crawl

No final words, no last goodbye
No gift given, taken tears subside

Challenges disappear
As if never here

World continues beyond my care
World exists despite me there

But I who live forever
Truth who never dies

Never born in splendor
Never lives in lies.

#YourLifetoo.

A revelation just came about my head
Do you really want what's coming your way.
G-d does not put
all his eggs in one basket
But if all good is what you want
Just go ahead and ask him

Then you will see
that all good does not come free
So you must be good yourself
In all you will be.
If you can do it
You will get what you want
If you get stuck
You will just have to hunt.

#universe

Time has no space
and space has no time
Space goes on to infinity
As time goes on beyond

Nothing really changes
But not ever stays the same
Only one thing we know
One day the source may show.

Only the unknown is certain
Only know for certain
one day we shall all perish
one day we may all be reborn.

I know no more than you
You know no more than I
School or streets, Alone we sleep
While only the universe survives

#see

Tell me my friend
  What do you see
Do you see the tears
That hide underneath

Tell me my enemy
  What do you see
Do you see the lion
That roars inside me

Tell me my love
  What do you see
Do you see the passion
That simmers to be

Tell me my teacher
  What do you see
Do you see the brilliance
You helped release

Tell me my mother
  What do you see
Do you see the heart
Only a mother can see

Tell me my father
  What do you see
Do you see the truth
Now that you are free

Tell me my G-D
  What do you see
Do you see the suffering
Now they BELIEVE.

#speakup

We sit and wait for the plague to pass
not knowing what rumbles below the ground
justice for one is injustice for all
but care not the ones at the top of the fall

greed bears many races
manipulation many faces
the cure to it call
peace and prosperity for all

until you who sits upon the fence
stand hand in hand with all else
the disparity between short and tall
will never cure the 'one for all'

we are but different 'all for one'
tell me who you think has won
quiet on the fence you stand in between
but greed has cleared the street you clean

dare to speak up you think not
for the fear of safety is on the spot
now or never is your turn
for your silence the streets will burn.

#challengeaccepted

I challenge you to change your pace
Fast to slow
and slow to fast
Perspective altered made to last

I challenge you to speak some truth
flattery left aside
From the heart and to the soul
connected we reside

I challenge you to befriend the lonely
Not popular at the very least
Nothing gained but a heart filled
And then you may pass the test

I challenge you to believe in G-d
Have faith in what's beyond
Give charity without glory
Let your name be what denies

I challenge you to say what you mean
Without fear or fury
Listen with an open heart
Change nothing but you only.

#savetheday

i was taught words have no impact
i have learned words can destroy
i was taught to follow and not speak out
i have learned to listen, speak and not be coy

i was taught elders always knew best
i have learned that experience can be a test
i was taught there's a right way and wrong
i have learned either way can be long
i was taught to believe what i've been told
i have learned without fear questions unfold
i was taught to bend over and stay
i have learned to walk away

i was taught to do no matter how it felt
i have learned important to take care of myself
i was taught to do it alone
i have learned asking for help is not wrong
i was taught to keep secrets and trust no one
i have learned to trust my friends and then some
i was taught the world is a dangerous place
i have learned freedom can save the day

#myhero

You were a giant in your own right
But still your absence remains
Your hand always extended
But still your absence remains
A hero some would say
But still your absence remains
all has left but a grave
But still your absence remains

Life's unfair lessons learned without complaints
But still your absence remains
The children continue to grow calling your name
But still your absence remains
Successes earned and failures triumph
But still your absence remains
Time just moves on
Still, your absence remains

Z"L NATAN BEN SHIMON

#"life is for the living"

A man is not made of stone
But of flesh.
A stone is forever
But has no life.
A life is made for the living.

Flesh alone will not make a man.
Man alone will not make a life.
A life is made for the living.

Time is spent, stones are gathered.
Life has passed by man.
A life is made for the living.

To see a glimmer of hope or truth.
Stones cast aside for man to see
a life is made for the living.

#time

Time does not keep me
I keep time.
sun rises
sun sets.
It is a day
because
I call it a day.
This precious thing
Wasted by all
Until
I see
Time does not keep me
I keep time.

#Creation

critics say beautiful art is born from intense pain.
artists say I was just trying to get out of the way.

I may never be among the great.
But I hold my head up high
and tried, I said.

I gave it all my honest best.

In a world of liars and cheats,
hustlers and whores
Rules none,

I turn my back and say no more.

Let karma sort it out
I lay down my sword
pick up my brush
create some more

no hurry, no rush,

no keeping score

The world my palette
Memories the paint
Stories hold the canvas
the light saves the pain.

B"H

#thehourofdeath

In the hour of death, what remains?

Nothing and yet everything.

Attachments, all discarded.

Not one to remain in our possession.

Not an eyelash. Not a finger or a nail.

Certainly not any bricks or mortar we enslaved ourselves for in the minutes we had plenty of.

And here, in the hour of death, the parasitic ego simply vanishes.

There is nothing left to eat from.

It has no medium to connect.

It is beaten, it is lost, it is forgotten.

And in that hour of death is the clarity we have sought for a lifetime that the ego kept interrupting.

From another perspective, it is the ego that has kept us alive this whole time.

For if we had the clarity sooner…. is when we have died.

'Flower of Life'

A SOUL'S TRUTH

#memories

I wonder where the memories go
When no one is left to call
Time moves forward
As does age
No one left to wonder the rage

Is there a place where they are all kept
A book, a space, a vision takes place
The soul remembers, what the mind forgets
But where do we go
Last night I got a call

The other side vibrant and clear
Healthy as any can be
This world just a disruption
No one knows
But all filled with corruption

Now time will pass for all to see
Choices made and prices paid
Fallen Angels finally freed
Memories stored and memoirs fade.

#survivor

A blink of an eye
And the world goes by
Moments of agony
overpaid for regret
unworthy Thinking
back to time wasted
and efforts ungained
Perfect we are not
But still nothing is a shame
Mistakes learned but
consequences prevail
Moving forward
a fairy tale
Truth unspoken but ever so real
The times we are quiet, the times we feel
A smile, a face, hands displaced
Time for courage at your pace
Perfect we are not
But worthy indeed
No one
Can ever make you bleed

#freedom

I wonder what words you read
The thoughts, are they free?
Do you share this out loud
Or hold your tongue, too proud

Do you fear others ways
Or does courage overtake?
Are you whole
Or partially void

Is it strategy that you fall to ground
But in the ballot box you rage?
Time to put yourself back in that cage
Others waiting you stay.

I dare you to speak as you wish
Make your inside be outlandish
Be true be honest be brave
Most of all never be swayed.

#tobuildorbrake

those who were controlled live by what is given
those who build alone are unforgiven
those who cannot build simply take
those who don't build at all simply brake

we who are living are dying
we who are dead come alive
we who are here are missing
we who are gone found survived

you who are lost travel far
you who are near can't be found
you who are hurt are forgiving
you who are sad have no bounds

i who am not born
i who cannot die
i who cannot live
i who am i

#challengemenot

what you did, it is not wrong
it is loving cunning shrewd quite strong
take what is yours don't look back
for a pillar of salt will become your pack
no justice no glory
no feeling of sorry's

challenge me not
for it is what you got
one day will come
where calm waters flow
then you will know where you will go

until that day
you will walk astray
picking up rocks along the way
the end unknown
for all who walk
this path alone

possible always is the change
see the light over the range
find the truth within yourself
fear subsides and nothing else
it is not real
none of what you see
all an illusion created by you and me

challenge me not
for it is what you got
one day will come
where calm waters flow
then you will know where you will go

B"H

#brokentogether

Twenty-twenty will be the year
That reminds us who shifts the gears
Control we lack but above all
Judgement time ready to call

We get this break a short reprieve
Before we are called to the one that sees
Sees all hears all nothing to hide
But one last chance to make it right

Mistakes made by many times two
But all are human with nothing to prove
The acts of love and suffering erase
All the mistakes that one may make

In the image of G-d we are all created
Forgiving loving compassionate yet jealous
It is our journey we strive to better
That one day we claim our letter

#lessonlearned

A mistake made is a lesson not forgotten
To the one whose heart is true
But suffer those who wallow in holes
Perfection A facade turned blue

Words spoken from the heart
may sometimes come out wrong
challenged by malicious intent
Will always appear mistakenly strong

Evil surrounds us That is for certain
goodness shall prevail
Days or decades it may take
karma will always set sail

Words are cheap actions speak louder
still you never know
Take a good look Surround yourself with love
And all else shall be found above.

#riches

Today I leave aside the riches
For a life simpler and plain
Full to the rim with love and tickles
Nothing less to remain

I make a choice solid and true
Hard for sure it turned me blue
But later will I know it through
But later will I see it bloom

There was a time I was alone
this time is not that at all
Prepared I am this time around
It is not I who will fall to ground

Cherish I do every minute spent
On what matters, love not rent
True are my words to speak
Gifts of glory do I seek

Take my hand Come to the light
Fear not, let worries subside
You are whole in the Lord's eyes
I am whole in the Lord's eyes.

#iamhere

I am here,
You are not alone
I am by your side

Through it all
It is hard,
Yes I know
Only pain

Can make you grow
This shell of yours
Is not to keep
too small for
what you seek

You were not born
To collect
Assets titles intellect

Allies enemies
too many to bare
Illusions all,
nothing really there

Unattach to what you know
all a matrix of the show
think not without reason
to every gain there is treason

challenges collapse counts
the end seemingly near
never
for i am here

B"H

About the Poet

The first poem I learned was in third grade, PS 174 in Forest Hills, NY. It was a Haiku. From that moment, I was hooked. I became fluent in the language of poetry. I would think in prose. It made total sense to me, more so than any other communication style. As an immigrant child I was attracted to the use of words without the limitations, restrictions and rules of grammar, of which I could not abide. It was like coloring outside the lines that was so liberating to me in my self-expression.

When I was young, communication came with its challenges. I didn't always succeed in saying what I meant in a colloquial and grammatically correct or even coherent manner. Filled with anxiety and shame, I stayed in the background just hoping to be liked, fearful of being seen and distressed over being excluded. But poetry, was always there for me and allowed me to just focus on the important words without the rules and judgment.

I started writing, all the time. Most people write to remember, *I write to forget*. Writing poems became a form of letting go for me whenever something horrible would happen to me or around me. But it also became a form of self-celebration. In lonely moments when I had no one to share the good news with and I was bursting out with emotions, the blank sheet was always a good friend. It held my secrets and my successes safely and this is where I learned how to trust in art.

Art is always true. It never lies. It never steals or cheats but will always reflect as it is entrusted. The more you give it the more it will grow. Even when you turn your back on it, it will always be there for you, just as you left it. no better no worse, always ready to move forward or stay where it is.

B"H

Like all things in life, you can't go back, you can't remove it, you can't take it away but you can always make it better.

And with every poem I wrote I started to learn to believe in myself. Some poems never made it to the paper, some never made it to the light of day, some discarded, some collected and some daringly shared.

The sharing my poetry is similar to walking across Madison Avenue naked. Without the support of my loving friends and husband I would have never dared to venture such an audacious act. I am blessed for all of the characters in my life. The ones I had to heal from and the ones that helped me heal.

I share this second book of poetry with all those that dare to live outside the lines that were drawn for you. I hope I inspire you to pick up a pen or a brush, to stroke a string or play a key and look deep within to feel the emotions that make us human; for in the words of Robin Williams in Dead Poet Society "Poetry is what we stay alive for." We are not alive to eat, learn, work, collect, shit and die. We are alive to feel all that our Creator has curated for us. Art is the method to reach our emotions and feel one with our creator while we are living. In the words of my late father and greatest teacher, life is for the living.

B"H

A Gift

Here I gift you with a blank page. It is yours to fill as you wish. A letter to be remembered, a gift to pass on, or a thought you have pondered for years on your journey across this Earth. You will reflect your thoughts and change the world, for it is only with words that we can evoke any transformation at all.

Inspired by Shakespeare, I leave you,

'To thine own **word** be true'.

B"H

...

ACKNOWLEDGEMENTS

There are many people who go to accomplish a task. There is no self-made man nor woman. It took a journey of experiences both loving and harsh to reveal the emotions within that we are destined to thrive from as well as heal from and evolve. On that note, to all those I've loved and who have loved me back, thank you for your unconditional support. To all those I loved and who did not love me back, thank you for my lessons learned, without which this book would have never been possible.

Thank you to my dear Synergy Education creators and classmates that uncovered a dream that I was too fearful to bring to consciousness on my own. Thank you to my writing class who developed my skill in your compassionate sharing and honest feedback.

Thank you Rudi, for the beautiful portrait you gifted me that opened my eyes to see the real me wading inside. It was the last piece of the puzzle that brought this whole promise to light. It was all as it is meant to be.

Lastly, thank you to my readers and supporters who believe in me and take a chance on an aspiration with a purpose to feel and heal.

B"H

A quote that has guided me through this healing journey...

"I trust that I can listen to my intuition. I can surrender.
I don't need to be in control of everything.
I know I am resilient and
capable of making a change,
if things need to change.
I know I will always show up for me."
-Jessica Ashley Gill, TBM

B"H

$26.00
ISBN 978-0-9916196-2-7

www.ingramcontent.com/pod-product-compliance
Lightning Source LLC
Chambersburg PA
CBHW060930180426
43192CB00044B/2843